ANDREW CUOMO: HIGHLIGHTS OF SEXUAL HARRASSMENT

CAN CUOMO ENDURE HIS PRESENT CHARGES

DAVID PATTERSON

TABLE OF CONTENTS

Introduction

Who Is Mr. Andrew Cuomo?

Mr. Cuomo, who has been a lead delegate for more than 10 years, is being explored from his own social event for purportedly disguising the veritable number of passings in New York care homes.

He is furthermore defying charges of torturing, including from the executive of New York City, and instances of improper conduct from a past assistant and various women

Andrew Engraving Cuomo considered December 6, 1957, is an American legislator, maker, and legitimate advocate filling in as the authoritative head of New York. A person from the Liberal union, he was picked for a comparable position his father, Mario Cuomo, held for three terms. He has filled in as seat of the Public Lead delegates Relationship since August 2020.

He is fundamental for a Vote based political practice - his late father was moreover a lead delegate and gigantically standard inside the social affair. Many requested that he run (twice) for president yet he denied.

His kin Chris is an early evening CNN anchor and he has chatted with his kin a couple of times. One exchange they shared when he was crippled with Covid was extensively shared.

Chapter One

What Has Cuomo Been Reprimanded For?

A sixth woman has leveled charges of unequivocally ill-advised direct against Gov. Andrew M. Cuomo, reprimanding him for reaching her without consent around the finish of a year ago during involvement with the lead agent's home, the Events Affiliation has confirmed.

The alleged event happened after the woman, a person from the lead agent's Main Chamber staff, had been called to the manor to assist the lead delegate with a business-related matter. The woman's chairmen actually got aware of the case and advised the lead delegate's leading group of it on Monday.

An authority close to the matter on Tuesday asserted to the Events Affiliation that the new case had been made, disregarding the way that Cuomo, during a news meeting hours afterward, held data back from getting it.

The woman moreover supposedly told the paper the lead agent reached her inappropriately on various occasions. She has not recorded a legitimate complaint.

Regardless, the paper definite that she taught a female executive concerning the scene after a social affair of staff people watched Mr Cuomo give a public meeting on 3 Walk forestalling past charges from getting incitement.

Cuomo: 'I never reached anyone inappropriately'

Mr. Cuomo was first reprimanded for goading in February, when Lindsey Boylan, a past undeniable level assistant, wrote in a piece that the lead agent reached her without her consent and a significant part of the time offered wrong comments about her appearance.

Ms. Boylan charged Mr. Cuomo with kissing her on the lips and mentioning that she plays strip poker while on his own extravagance plane.

Another past partner, Charlotte Bennett, told the New York Times that she grasped the lead delegate expected to set down with me.

Chapter Two

Cuomo: New York Lead Delegate Rebellious As More Liberals Encourage Him To Resign

Andrew Cuomo has requested he will not notification calls to stop as New York lead delegate over charges of sexual offense.

He was by then being analyzed after grumblings from five women and is presently defying charges of assault from a sixth.

New York lawmakers Alexandria Ocasio-Cortez and Jerry Nadler are the latest nonconformists mentioning that he adventure down.

The New York lead agent has kept all from getting the cases against him.

Mr. Cuomo underlined he would not leave in an approach Friday.

I didn't do what has been guaranteed, he said. I never bullied anyone, I never assaulted anyone, I never misused anyone.

Earlier, Ms. Ocasio-Cortez and Agent Jamaal Bowman conveyed a joint clarification that said, we acknowledge these women, we acknowledge the reporting, we acknowledge the Head legitimate official, and we acknowledge the 55 people from the New York State get together.

Lead agent Cuomo can now don't effectively lead even with such endless troubles, the attestation said.

New York City Director Bill de Blasio, a drawn-out political adversary of Radical Lead delegate Cuomo, told reporters on Thursday that the latest charge is "disgusting to me, and he can now don't fill in as a lead agent.

I'm not going to leave. I was not picked by the public authority authorities. I was picked by people, Mr. Cuomo responded on Friday evening.

Mr. Cuomo, whose term in office arrives at a determination in 2022, was a year prior acclaimed for his treatment of the Covid plague in his state. In any case, this year he has been censured for obscuring the size of Coronavirus passings in the state's nursing homes. Since the charges of incitement were caused a progression of people have required his renunciation.

On Thursday, New York State Get-together Speaker Carl Heastie said he had offered the go-ahead for an arraignment assessment into the cases made against Mr. Cuomo. The assessment, which will chat with witnesses and look at the evidence, would be the underlying move towards condemnation.

More than 55 Notoriety based heads in New York have denoted a letter moving toward him to wander down.

In an attestation Mr. Cuomo called the new cases, uncovered by the Events Relationship of Albany on Wednesday, "horrible".

He has as of late said that he would hold on for the outcomes of a self-sufficient assessment concerning the charges, which is being regulated by New York's essential legitimate official Letitia James.

Chapter Three

Charges of Hide by Cuomo Over Nursing Home Disease Cost

Gov. Andrew M. Cuomo and his association faced new charges that they had disguised the degree of the Coronavirus death toll in New York's nursing homes, after a top partner to the lead delegate yielded that the state had held data since it feared an assessment by the Trump Value Office.

The remarks by the top assistant, Melissa DeRosa, made in what ought to be a private call with Greater part rule authorities, came as a falling course of action of data reports and a court demand have left Mr. Cuomo, a third-term radical, scrambling to contain the political fallout over his oversight of nursing homes, where more than 13,000 people have passed on in the pandemic in the state.

Over 33% of U.S. Coronavirus Passings Are Associated with Nursing Homes

The contamination has squashed tenants and staff people more than 31,000 long stretch consideration workplaces the country over.

Lawmakers from the two players have called for stripping the authoritative top of the emergency controls that he has worked on during the pandemic, while moderates have mentioned the acquiescences of top Cuomo association specialists and new government assessments.

We were in a position where we didn't know whether what we intended to accommodate the Division of Value, or what we accommodate all of you, and what we start saying, would have been used against us and we didn't know whether there would have been an assessment, Ms. DeRosa said during the call, according to a midway record later conveyed by the lead delegate's office after her remarks appeared in The New York Post.

The Value Office never formally opened an assessment, as shown by Ms. DeRosa. However, the outstanding assessment of the lead delegate's record on nursing homes has struck at the focal point of his carefully evolved picture as a capable President with an admission to real factors, as embodied constantly by-day news get-togethers that he held consistently in the scene. Mr. Cuomo even dispersed a diary about his work on the pandemic before it got done with, offering activity works out.

The procedure with requests in regards to the quantity of people passed on in nursing home tenants finds a way ways to obscure Mr. Cuomo's legacy.

Just fourteen days earlier, the state's head lawful official, Letitia James, who has been an accomplice of the lead delegate, in a censuring report reprimanded the Cuomo association for undercounting Coronavirus related passings related with nursing homes in gigantic numbers.

Chapter Four

The Political Ground Is Breaking down Under Andrew Cuomo's Feet

The most critical situation for the New York lead delegate was predictable that the early revelations about his direct in office would provoke new wrong conduct sources, revealing an illustration of direct.

That has every one of the reserves of being happening, and even more New York government authorities are organizing against Cuomo.

The flood of the state administrative radicals requiring Cuomo's renouncement on Friday is just the latest, most immense unforeseen development.

A part of the names included are self-evident. Alexandria Ocasio-Cortez and Jamaal Bowman, for instance, are reformists who unseated Cuomo-maintained officeholder nonconformists.

The uprising against Cuomo isn't limited aside flank, regardless. It joins House Legitimate chief Seat Jerrold Nadler - a sign that Cuomo is losing the assistance of his social occasion's establishment, too.

In every one of them, 11 of the state's 19 House liberals are presently on the record requiring Cuomo's renunciation, close by many state authorities. As the copy of the assessment, the strain on the plague lead delegate is creating.

Chapter Five

Six Highlights From The Cuomo Sexual Harassment Scandal

Here are the main six highlights from the continuous outrage up until this point:

1. The NY Head legal officer's Office was given a reference to autonomously explore the lewd behavior claims

On Monday, March 1, New York Head legal officer Letitia James said her office got a reference letter from the leader chamber giving her position to autonomously examine the cases of inappropriate behavior against the Lead representative. The reference likewise gives the AG's office summon power.

She said in a statement: the leader chamber sent a reference letter to our office, giving us the power to push ahead with a free examination concerning charges of lewd behavior claims made against Lead representative Cuomo. This isn't an obligation we trifle with as charges of inappropriate behavior ought to consistently be viewed appropriately. As the letter states, at the end of the survey, the discoveries will be revealed in a public report."

NEW YORK Head legal officer LETITIA JAMES

Chief approves Principal legal officer to research Cuomo

2. Cuomo apologizes for activities, claims they were 'confused'

In an articulation Sunday, Gov. Cuomo said a portion of his activities may have been "confounded as an undesirable tease." He said he had prodded individuals about their own lives trying to be "perky" yet that he never intended to hurt anybody.

He said to some degree:

I presently comprehend that my communications may have been obtuse or excessively close to home and that a portion of my remarks, given my position, caused others to feel in manners I won't ever expect. I recognize a portion of the things I have said have been misjudged as an undesirable tease. To the degree anybody felt that way, I'm really grieved about that.

NEW YORK GOV. ANDREW CUOMO

The Lead representative kept up that he never improperly contacted anybody nor propositioned anybody.

His subsequent informer impugned the statement of regret.

Cuomo sorry for comments helper 'confused' as badgering

3. The Lead representative's Office at first chose a previous government judge to direct the examination

The New York Head legal officer's Office intends to enlist a law office and select an exceptional agent to explore the badgering charges, however this solitary comes after the Lead representative's Office recently recommended a government judge with connections to his organization to lead the examination.

Saturday night, the Cuomo organization reported previous Government Judge Barbara Jones would lead an audit of the badgering claims, however they got reaction over the morals of the Lead representative picking his own commentator.

Cuomo's office at that point proposed the head legal officer and the Central Adjudicator of the Court of Advances together select an "free and qualified attorney in private practice without political connection" to direct the audit.

Principal legal officer James at that point mentioned a reference, including summon powers from the Lead representative, so she can "direct that examination and make any arrangements vital." She additionally delivered an ensuing explanation expressing she dismissed Cuomo's proposition of an examination headed by an autonomous lawyer.

To explain, I don't acknowledge the Lead representative's proposition. The state's Chief Law plainly gives my office the position to examine this matter once the Lead representative gives a reference. While I have profound regard for Boss Adjudicator DiFiore, I'm the appropriately chosen Principal legal officer and it is my obligation to do this assignment, per Leader Law. The Lead representative should give this reference so an autonomous examination with summon force can be directed."

NEW YORK Principal legal officer LETITIA JAMES

She was at last given the reference on Monday.

Principal legal officer and Lead representative's Office conflict over provocation survey

4. A subsequent lady blames Cuomo for lewd behavior

A second previous associate blamed the Lead representative for lewd behavior in a meeting with The New York Times. Charlotte Bennett, 25, claims Cuomo, 63, posed her inquiries about her sexual coexistence, including on the off chance that she had at any point been with a more seasoned man. The previous wellbeing strategy counselor likewise expressed the Lead representative said he was "available to associations with ladies in their 20s."

Second lady blames Lead representative Cuomo for inappropriate behavior

5.   Previous   assistant   blames   the   Lead representative for inappropriate behavior

Lindsey Boylan, 36, first charged Gov. Cuomo of inappropriate behavior in a tweet in December 2020.

She followed up her allegation with a piece she composed on Medium in February that itemized affirmed badgering she said she encountered while working for the Lead representative. In the article, she blamed Cuomo for proposing they play strip poker while on his personal luxury plane and kissing her after a gathering.

Cuomo has denied her cases.

Previous assistant says Cuomo kissed her, recommended strip poker

6. Expanding number of officials call for examination, Lead representative's acquiescence

In the midst of the lewd behavior charges, an expanding number of officials on the two sides of the passageway are on the side of an autonomous examination, and many are requiring Cuomo's renunciation.

The Vote based New York Senate Dominant part Pioneer said the proceeded with claims are profoundly upsetting and concerning," and the Conservative Senate Minority Pioneer said "I have been vocal in requiring a finish to the Lead representative's crisis powers, something I still unequivocally support. However, considering the information on the previous few weeks, it has become progressively evident that doesn't go far enough.

Chapter Six

Conclusion

Sometime the state's two Vote based administrators, including astounding bigger part pioneer Throw Schumer, should say something - either to throw him a lifeline or, possibly, pass on the last blow.

Cuomo recently was encountering reputation trouble with a crisis related to his association's attested concealment of data related to Covid passings in nursing homes. Requires his quiet submission are flooding in from people from his own social event, and the calls of stun create more grounded reliably. Different parts set it apart and will make it harder for him to restore his standing or look for higher office.

Five separate claims of lecherous conduct — four from women who worked with Cuomo — further enhanced the negative blowback that for the most part existed.

In any case, sex shocks are savage burst; they don't burn-through continuously.

Dynamically, the request will become: Can adequate New York liberals get seared to some degree to offer cover to help Cuomo hold tight in Albany?

In the time of electronic media, that could exhibit problematically.

By and large hurting of all, perhaps, is the photo verification — and the ensuing pictures. News sources have run a photo of Cuomo putting his hands on the substance of an unassuming, young woman. The lighting is enthusiastic. The woman's non-verbal correspondence seems to signal alert and misery. While giving no confirmation, fundamentally, of awful conduct, the photo cements an image of Cuomo bearing a surge — because, clearly, it has been changed into electronic media pictures. At the point when that happens, the horde of people who consider the charges against you develops unfathomably — and the "message" gets hard to regulate.

Cuomo is an expert administrator who appears to have made staggers he should have known to sidestep. Also, he can't ensure these alleged events were imperfections from his youth: They all are really later.

www.ingramcontent.com/pod-product-compliance
Lightning Source LLC
Chambersburg PA
CBHW060931130726
48001CB00006B/2527